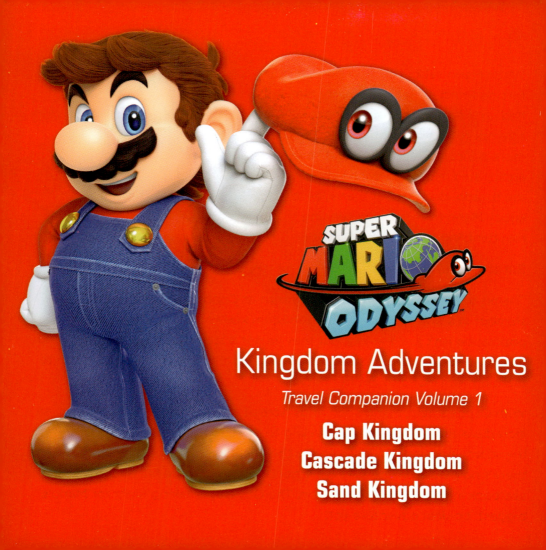

SUPER MARIO ODYSSEY

Kingdom Adventures

Travel Companion Volume 1

Cap Kingdom
Cascade Kingdom
Sand Kingdom

Pack Your Bags!

When Mario set out to stop Bowser from forcing Princess Peach to marry him, he had no idea what it would lead to. But his attempt to save a friend quickly proves far more difficult than Mario could have ever anticipated. Much to Peach's dismay, the tuxedo-clad Bowser manages to knock Mario from his ship, sending him tumbling through the night sky.

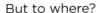

But to where?

Thanks to a friendly flying top hat known as Cappy, Mario is roused from his slumber in a tiny area of the Cap Kingdom known as Bonneton. The local population isn't just friendly, but they've got a stake in stopping Bowser too! One of their own, Cappy's sister Tiara, was also kidnapped, and he wants to team up with Mario to get her back.

With Cappy's help, Mario soon finds himself in command of the Odyssey, an incredible airship capable of traveling to more than a dozen kingdoms. From the scorching sands of Tostarena to the bustling streets of New Donk City, there's no place the Odyssey can't go. Don your favorite hat and put your seatback in its full, upright position. The Odyssey is taking flight for Mario's biggest, boldest adventure yet!

CONTINUE THE ADVENTURE!

Collect all six volumes of *Super Mario Odyssey: Kingdom Adventures* to follow Mario on his epic journey!

Mario's desire to stop Bowser may be his ultimate goal, but the best part of any adventure is the journey, not the destination. And oh, the places you'll go, Mario!

Take us along as we help you uncover the secrets of the first three kingdoms in Mario's quest. The following pages contain insights into the most popular tourist attractions, regional events and activities, local culture, and souvenirs. Consider this book your ultimate travel companion, a tour guide designed to not only help you get the most out of your travels, but also a record of the memorable times you and Mario share.

This volume provides insights into the Cap Kingdom, Cascade Kingdom, and Sand Kingdom. For gameplay assistance, maps of Power Coins, and general strategy, be sure to check out the *Official Super Mario Odyssey Strategy Guide*, sold separately.

Cap Kingdom

Home of Tradition, Propriety, and Hats

From the moment Mario lands in the Cap Kingdom, it's clear that this world of felt and fog is unlike any he's ever seen. Though all of the gray and black may seem a bit gloomy at first, Bonneton is a delight to visit thanks to the colorful inhabitants.

Across the hills and undulating bridge lies a small town of friendly locals known as Bonneters, named after this island town. While many choose to live in the Central Plaza, others have opted to live atop the impressive Top-Hat Tower. Do pay them a visit!

Ringed by a distant skyline containing hundreds of buildings, many adorned with top hats, the local Bonneters go about their lives manufacturing all manner of hat-inspired creations. From the homes they live in, to the airships they sail upon, the Bonneters have a love of all things hat-shaped. Even the currency resembles a top hat!

Life in Bonneton is simple and safe, with few threats ever coming to the floating Bonneters. Even the few Paragoombas that flutter around the area seem to pose no problem.

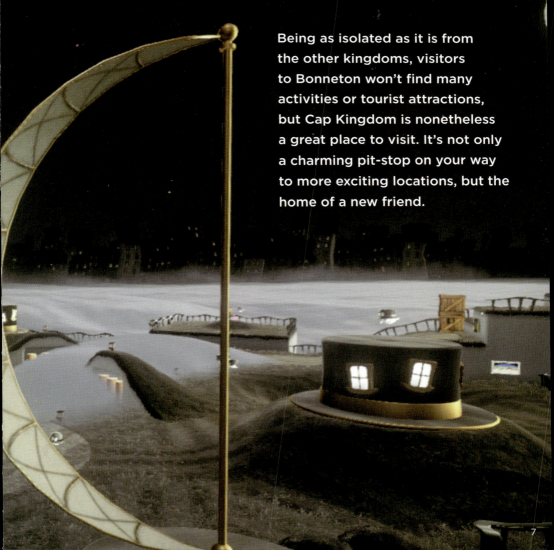

Being as isolated as it is from the other kingdoms, visitors to Bonneton won't find many activities or tourist attractions, but Cap Kingdom is nonetheless a great place to visit. It's not only a charming pit-stop on your way to more exciting locations, but the home of a new friend.

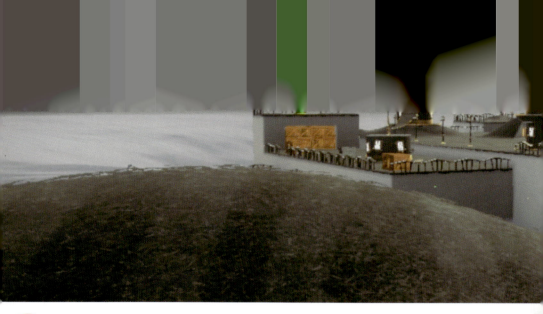

Bonneton

A land of haberdashed dreams

GET TO KNOW BONNETON	
Population	Middling
Size	Smallish
Locals	Bonneters
Currency	Hat-Shaped
Industry	Hats, Airships
Temperature	Average 71°F

The Bonneters of Cap Kingdom are among the friendliest of everyone Mario meets on his journey. These little creatures are never without their trademark hats—top hats for the men and bowler hats for the ladies—and can be seen floating throughout the region.

THREE KEYS TO THE KINGDOM

 Appreciate the distinctive architectural style based on hat silhouettes.

 Enjoy the romantic glow of the moonlit, fog-shrouded streets.

 Chat with the kind and ever-courteous Bonneters.

Top Sights

World's Best Hat Stand

This eye-catching tower is famous in Bonneton, both as a landmark itself and for the spectacular view from the "brim."

Visitors are allowed inside, but many creatures call the tower home, much to the surprise of first timers.

Does it fit my head? #Bonneton, #BigHats, #WhoLetTheFrogsOut

GONE TO THE FROGS

Mario will never forget Cappy helping him perform his very first capture inside this tower. Who knew frogs could leap so high?!

One day, I want to live in a hat wearing a hat. #TopThis #Bonneton, #Accessorize

Extremely Mobile Homes

Notice the unique dwellings shaped like hats. These constructions double as both house and airship for the Bonneters, who take great pride in them.

Some of the larger "houseboats" even have two stories. As private dwellings, you can't just stroll inside, but the natives don't mind people climbing on top of their homes. Perhaps being atop private property comes naturally to these hat-like people.

HAVE NO FEAR

The Bonneters are a courageous bunch. They don't seem afraid of anything. Except Paragoombas. This little fellow is terrified of Paragoombas!

A Spectacle of a Bridge

The bridge that connects the central square and the hills is called Glasses Bridge. It's a long, double-arched structure whose bottom is hidden in a sea of clouds. When you see it, you'll understand its affectionate nickname immediately. Many tourists enjoy the speedy thrill of rolling across the undulating structure—be sure to give it a try.

Wheee! #DizzySpell #Bonneton #GlassesBridge

Old-Fashioned Lighting

These unique lights only appear in Bonneton. Since the area gets so dark every time the moon goes behind the clouds, the lights are designed to be switched on with a simple turn of the lantern.

Advanced lightbulb changing. #Fit4Life #TheWorldIsYourGym #Bonneton

The elegant design of these lampposts draws many tourists. They're even lovelier when turned on, so do give each one a spin as you pass by.

BEST TRAVEL BUDDIES

Who knew a hat could become such a wonderful travel companion? Mario didn't know what to expect at first, but he's sure glad he met Cappy atop Glasses Bridge.

FREE COINS

Mario was thrilled to discover he could earn coins from most of the lanterns he turned on. Fortunately, Cappy didn't mind since the lanterns look like hat racks.

TFW you remember roller coasters make you nauseous.
#Bonneton #SometimesBridge #NotFeelingSoWell

Sometimes Bridge was true to its name when Mario first tried to cross it. Lucky for him, Cappy has quite a grip and was able to pull the lever to raise it.

The "Sometimes" Bridge

The bridge connecting Central Square to Top-Hat Tower is built to retract in an emergency. If this happens during your visit, don't panic—just use the switch to restore the bridge.

It's-a-You, Here!

The Odyssey: The locals call this area "The Hills" because it's super bumpy. It's a great place to land the Odyssey.

Central Plaza: This is where the Bonneters like to live. It's a great spot to go souvenir shopping!

Top-Hat Tower: The brim of Top-Hat Tower is so large, a lot of Bonneters built their homes atop it.

Souvenir Hunting

The Bonneters love of hats extends to their currency. There are 50 hat-shaped coins scattered throughout Cap Kingdom, waiting to be found. They can earn Mario fancy new duds and souvenirs.

CRAZY CAP: BONNETON EXCLUSIVES	
ITEM	**REGIONAL COINS**
Black Top Hat	5
Black Tuxedo	10
Cap Kingdom Sticker	5
Plush Frog	5
Bonneton Tower Model	25

HAZARDS & HOSTILES

Bonneton is the safest, friendliest place Mario visits during his journey. From the soft padding of the felt underfoot to the near absence of hostile creatures, it's a great place to wander without fear. Of course, no place is completely safe from danger. Bonneton has two specific things to watch out for.

Paragoomba: These winged cousins of the Goomba are less aggressive than their ground-based brethren, but they can still do Mario harm if he bumps into them. It's best to let them continue their endless patrol uninterrupted.

Sea of Clouds: The biggest danger in Cap Kingdom is falling. Those clouds might look like pillows, but they won't catch you if you take a spill. Stick to solid ground—or the trusted wings of a Paragoomba—to avoid injury. Fortunately, this threat really only applies to those wishing to visit the sunken hats off the coast of Bonneton.

Aside from the Paragoomba and the Binoculars in Central Plaza, Bonneton has very few local inhabitants that can be captured. But the one Mario can capture sure can hop!

Frog: Frogs can be found near The Hills and inside Top-Hat Tower. Mario won't encounter another creature anywhere that can leap as high as a frog.

Events and Attractions

Koopa Freerunning

The Roving Racers hold freerunning events on the brim of Top-Hat Tower. Can you beat the Koopas to the tallest hill near the Odyssey? The key to getting there first is to roll, roll, roll like you've never rolled before!

Postcards with Peach

There's nothing quite like running into friends while traveling. Mario can experience this joy in Central Plaza, where Peach awaits. Why not take a photo with her in front of the full moon?

Local Advice

Shadow Play

Always pay attention to the shadows cast on the ground, as they often indicate rings, platforms, or collectibles that you may not otherwise see. Sometimes the tiniest of shadows is your only clue that a ? Block or purple coin is floating high above.

Cascade Kingdom

Land of Waterfalls and Natural Treasures

Whether it's your first visit to Cascade Kingdom or your tenth, the majestic Great Falls and prehistoric scenery never fail to impress. Cascade Kingdom is a vibrant, grass-covered mountainside, nestled in a basin surrounded by towering waterfalls.

Though this former land of cavemen and dinosaurs boasts no advanced civilization, the signs of its early inhabitants are everywhere. Marvel at the fossils embedded within the rocks, wonder at the cloud-like platforms that expand when struck, and gaze upon the massive fossils that dot the landscape.

Cascade Kingdom is one of the tallest landscapes Mario visits in his travels. Conquer your fear of heights as you balance your way across Stone Bridge and scale the mighty Ancient Wall in an effort to reach the region's highest point.

Fossil Falls may be the land that time forgot, but it's not without life. While creatures big and small continue to make their home here, the biggest draw is the mighty Tyrannosaurus Rex. Fortunately for visitors, the docile T-Rex spends nearly all of his time napping—and isn't disturbed by camera flashes.

Though tourism in Fossil Falls has yet to rival that of nearby Tostarena, the Bonneters have opened a Crazy Cap store in the region in hopes of attracting future business. Now, if only the Chain Chomps were interested in souvenirs...

Fossil Falls

The last holdout of history

GET TO KNOW FOSSIL FALLS	
Population	Unknown
Size	Tall
Locals	Unknown
Currency	Stone Disks
Industry	Unknown
Temperature	Average 84°F

THREE KEYS TO THE KINGDOM

1 *Experience the glory of nature with eye-popping Great Falls.*

2 *See dinosaurs, prehistoric rulers of a bygone age.*

3 *Find treasures of the past, tucked away everywhere you look.*

NO INTELLIGENT LIFE

Cascade Kingdom is one of the very few kingdoms Mario visits that doesn't have a local population. Though the occasional Toad or Koopa may visit once peace returns, the region is without a host civilization.

Sometimes you just have to ask yourself: Did cavemen have shampoo? #RIPtriceratops, #TravelInspiration, #FossilFalls

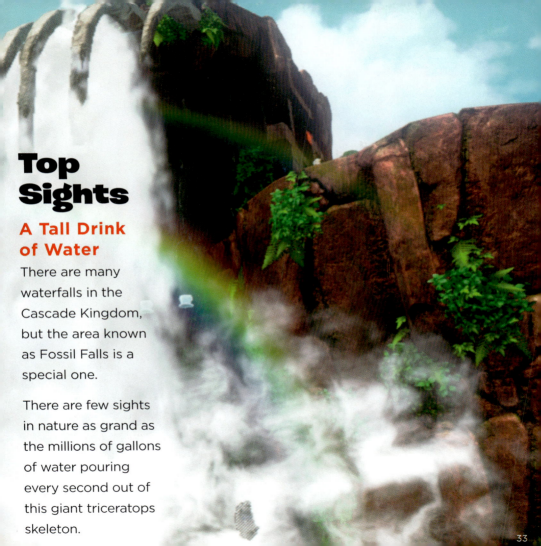

Top Sights

A Tall Drink of Water

There are many waterfalls in the Cascade Kingdom, but the area known as Fossil Falls is a special one.

There are few sights in nature as grand as the millions of gallons of water pouring every second out of this giant triceratops skeleton.

Nature in Balance

The stone spire standing near the great falls has miraculously remained balanced upright in this position, presumably for eons.

Of particular interest are the cubes of unknown material embedded in the stone. These cubes are the reason for the common theory that the spire fell from the sky. While this theory is difficult to prove, it is equally hard to doubt when looking at this miraculous structure.

I think I broke it. #Oops #FossilFalls, #NaturalBridge

THE FIRST POWER MOON

Mario will feed hundreds of Power Moons into the Odyssey by the time his journey is complete, but he'll always remember his first. Too bad about the stone spire.

The Ancient Wall

This structure was carved out painstakingly over many long years by people unknown. The wall is composed mainly of fossils, and evidence suggests it has been broken many times, causing some to suggest that something is buried inside.

The Ancient Wall didn't just contain fossils, but a working, fully-functional ode to Mario's early beginnings. Enter the 8-bit pipe for a brief sample of the past.

Magical times spent with two buttons. #NES4EVA #8BitFTW #FossilFalls

37

The Prehistoric Tyrant

The biggest draw for tourists is that dinosaurs still live here. T-Rex, most terrible of all dinosaurs, can pulverize a boulder with a single blow. On the other hand, most people don't realize how much time they spend napping.

Don't try this at home, I'm a professional. #DinoDinner #T-Rex #FossilFalls

BURRBO EXTERMINATION

Sure, a T-Rex can be used to smash blocks and knock aside Chain Chomps, but did you know they can also exterminate rainbow-colored pests like Burrbos? They can! But only between naps.

An Old, Odd Structure

No one knows how a Bonneton-style structure got buried here. Bonneters travel often, so they may have lived here in the past.

A little old, but it runs great! #BonneterTech, #AirshipLife #Odyssey #FossilFalls

UP AND AWAY

The Odyssey may have looked like a fossilized top hat, but it was actually one of the Bonneter's airships. And boy did it sparkle with a full suite of Power Moons!

The Odyssey: The Odyssey lands in an area known as Waterfall Basin, prized for being one of the only spots where visitors can view a double rainbow over the waterfall.

2

Top of the Big Stump: *The only known way to this plateau is via a pipe hidden behind a fossilized wall.*

3

Island in the Sky: *Art fans can reach this mysterious place via a magical portal in Lake Kingdom. Sadly, there's no other way to reach it.*

4

Stone Bridge: *The colorful Burrbos that inhabit Stone Bridge aren't as cute as they first appear.*

Fossil Falls Heights: *Scale the 8-bit level to reach the highest point in Fossil Falls and gain an up-close view of the triceratops skeleton.*

5

Getting Around

Warp points are great, but they're not the only way to get around. Put a little zap in Mario's step by capturing the Spark Pylon atop the electrical pole near the Odyssey. This can deliver Mario to the top of Fossil Falls Heights zippity quick!

Souvenir Hunting

Purple coins in the shape of stone disks are scattered throughout the region. Those entrepreneurial Bonneters from nearby Cap Kingdom have set up a shop where you can spend them. Take home some souvenirs and a very retro Caveman Outfit.

CRAZY CAP: FOSSIL FALLS EXCLUSIVES	
ITEM	REGIONAL COINS
Caveman Headwear	5
Caveman Outfit	10
Cascade Kingdom Sticker	5
T-Rex Model	5
Triceratops Trophy	25

HAZARDS & HOSTILES

You might think visiting an uncivilized prehistoric environment would be full of grave danger, but Cascade Kingdom is generally fairly safe. Sure, there's the ever-present risk of falling off the edge of a cliff, but the primary risks aren't terribly life-threatening.

Chain Chomp: The biggest threat facing visitors are the Chain Chomps that populate Waterfall Basin and Fossil Falls Heights. Fortunately, their chains have been bolted to the ground.

Burrbo: These colorful spikey creatures may look friendly, but they're surprisingly aggressive. Let Cappy clear the path for you. And whatever you do, don't ground pound them. Ouch!

Over the Falls: *Visitors to Fossil Falls should worry about more than just falling off the edge of the kingdom. The water's flowing fast and even a world-class swimmer like Mario can be swept away if not careful.*

CAPTIVE FRIENDSHIPS

Not many of the inhabitants of Cascade Kingdom can be captured, but what they don't have in numbers, they more than make up for in size. Aside from the Chain Chomps mentioned previously, Mario can also capture a living, breathing (snoring?) dinosaur.

T-Rex: *The history books never mentioned how much time a Tyrannosaurus Rex spends napping. Who knew? As fun as it is to climb on top of it, it's even more fun to capture one. Dino smash!*

47

ROCKBLOCK REMOVAL

Nobody likes a roadblock, not even when it's a fossil conglomerate. Lucky for Mario, there's two great ways to remove the blocks at Fossil Falls. One way is to wind a Chain Chomp up and let it fly. That can be a lot of fun. But you know what's even more fun? Taking control of your very own T-Rex!

Events and Attractions

Koopa Freerunning

The Roving Racers hold races all across the globe, including in Cascade Kingdom.

Chat with the Koopa near the Odyssey once races resume to challenge his fellow Koopas to the base of the Ancient Wall (or what's left of it).

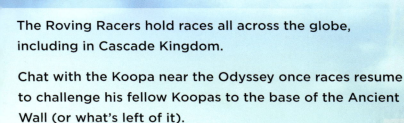

Postcards with Peach

Peach and Tiara are in Cascade Kingdom the same time as Mario. Small world! Ascend Fossil Falls Heights to say hi—or is it high—and take a snapshot with her for old time's sake.

Art Appreciation

What a strange place to find such fine art! Mario was swimming beneath the Great Falls when he stumbled upon a cave containing a painting. The first time he visited the area, the canvas was blank. But, on a return trip, the image took form. It looked an awful lot like one of the most dangerous airborne kingdoms he ever saw.

Local Advice

Forever Super Mario

Fans of the older *Super Mario Bros* games may expect Mario to shrink in size when hit by a Goomba inside an 8-bit level, but he won't. His health segments still apply inside the 8-bit levels. Mario stays nice and super-sized so long as he has health.

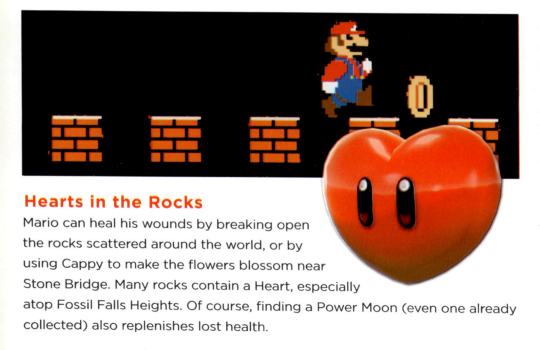

Hearts in the Rocks

Mario can heal his wounds by breaking open the rocks scattered around the world, or by using Cappy to make the flowers blossom near Stone Bridge. Many rocks contain a Heart, especially atop Fossil Falls Heights. Of course, finding a Power Moon (even one already collected) also replenishes lost health.

Sand Kingdom

Home of Red Sands and Lively Locals

If the prior stops on Mario's journey felt a little small, or the attractions a bit limited, then you're in for a treat! Sand Kingdom isn't just the sandiest tourist destination in the world, it's the hottest too. Literally!

Pack your sunscreen, break out your sombrero, and drink plenty of water, as the red-hot world of Tostarena is no place to travel unprepared. This expansive region of desert, ruins, and poisonous pools extends as far as Cappy's eyes can see—and you'll want to traverse every inch of it to get your coins' worth!

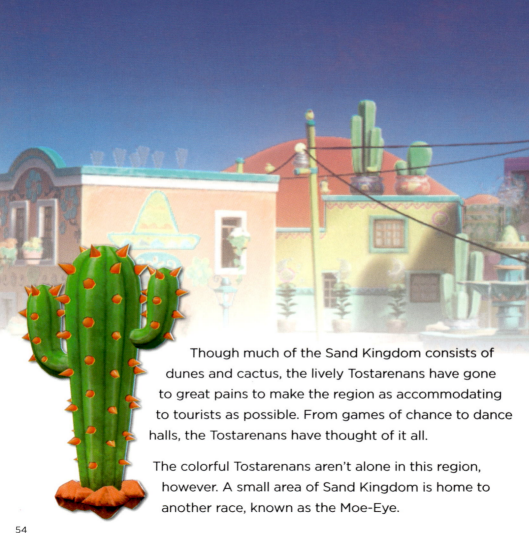

Though much of the Sand Kingdom consists of dunes and cactus, the lively Tostarenans have gone to great pains to make the region as accommodating to tourists as possible. From games of chance to dance halls, the Tostarenans have thought of it all.

The colorful Tostarenans aren't alone in this region, however. A small area of Sand Kingdom is home to another race, known as the Moe-Eye.

Considerably less savvy in the world of tourism, the Moe-Eye possess an ability the Tostarenans can only dream of. Let's just say, you'll have to see it to believe it!

Whether you come for the ruins, the waters of the oasis, or the desert solitude, you're sure to find something worth remembering. So, park the Odyssey and stay for a while. But bring a good map, you don't want to get lost out there.

Tostarena

Gateway to the stark beauty of the desert

GET TO KNOW TOSTARENA	
Population	Middling
Size	Expansive
Locals	Tostarenans, Moe-Eyes
Currency	Pyramid-shaped
Industry	Tourism, precious stones
Temperature	Average 104°F

SHAKE YOUR MARACAS!

The party-loving Tostarenans know how to make a visitor welcome. From their lively, upbeat attitude, to their penchant for offering travel advice whenever needed, they're always there to help.

THROWIN' SHADE

Tucked away in an isolated area in the west of Sand Kingdom reside the Moe-Eye. These gentle, stone creatures are the largest of all local populations, but also the most timid. Moe-Eye run at the first sight of a visitor, so getting close can be tough. The Moe-Eye are never without their special sunglasses and, unlike the Tostarenans, Mario and Cappy can capture one to check out the view.

THREE KEYS TO THE KINGDOM

 Enjoy the small but lively desert village and its charming inhabitants.

 Wonder at the Inverted Pyramid and its upside-down magic.

 Watch for the gem iconography carved in relief on the ruins.

Top Sights

Tostarenan Tourism

A small town that serves as the hub for tourists planning to visit the Inverted Pyramid. The colorful buildings and cheerful people provide a warm welcome for visitors. They're happy to provide direction, so don't hesitate to say hello.

This airship brakes for shaved ice! #LocalEats, #TasteTheWorld, #Tostarena

TRAVELERS ABOUND

Tostarena is the hottest travel destination this side of the Mushroom Kingdom. Literally! Expect to meet citizens from around the globe as you seek shade from the sweltering sun.

Mysterious Ancient Ruins

North of town you find ancient ruins dotting the expansive desert, many of which are patrolled by Bullet Bills.

Your eye is drawn to the large stone tower at the heart of the ruins. Due to extensive hollowing underground, quicksand has become prevalent in this area, so watch out.

The arch is amazing! So much bigger in person.
#Tostarena #TravelInspiration, #AncientRuins

Inverted Pyramid

The true "can't miss" of this region, the Inverted Pyramid may look unstable, but rest assured it never topples and has thrilled tourists for years. It is said that the legendary artifact called the Binding Band lies within, and the upside-down pyramid symbolizes how those joined by it will never part even if the world turns upside down.

Nothing to see here, just a pyramid balancing on a hat.
#InvertedPyramid, #ROFL #Tostarena

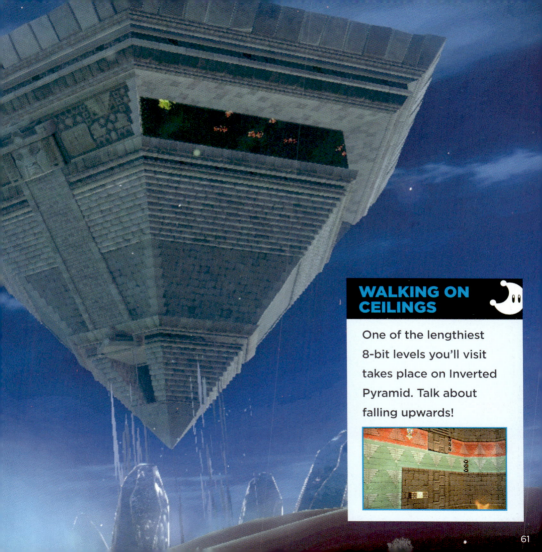

WALKING ON CEILINGS

One of the lengthiest 8-bit levels you'll visit takes place on Inverted Pyramid. Talk about falling upwards!

Jaxi

Hop on the back of the curious local transport, known as the Jaxi, and you'll be in for a wild, but completely reliable, ride.

Woah, Jaxi! WOAH! #HitTheBrakes #RunawayJaxi #Tostarena

RUNNING ON POISON

The purple wastes surrounding Jaxi Ruins are no threat to the fleet-footed beast. Hop aboard Jaxi and take off across the poison pond without fear.

Mental note: Don't forget to pack swimwear next time. #JustKeepSwimming, #DesertOasis, #Tostarena

Living Heart of the Desert

Here's a spot to moisten your dried and withered heart, with greenery and water to make you forget you're in the desert. The fish and birds are plentiful and well worth a visit.

FISHING WITH LAKITU

Most visitors don't think to bring their fishing pole when they come to Sand Kingdom, but the Desert Oasis is well-stocked with Cheep Cheeps. Try tossing your cap at Lakitu and see what you can reel in.

Legend has it there's a mighty big fish in this pond.

BIRDS OF THE KINGDOM

Two large birds can be seen circling the desert, forever in search of something to eat—or a tourist wanting to toss a hat at them. Of course, there are plenty of little birds too. Ever wonder if they land on that bump for a reason?

It's-a-You, Here!

The Odyssey: The Odyssey lands on the southern edge of the desert, not far from the hustle and bustle of Tostarena Town.

Tostarena Town: *The gateway town to the desert sights is home to a lively crowd of merchants, souvenir hawkers, and shaved ice salesman all waiting to help tourists spend their money.*

Desert Oasis: *Whether you want to go swimming, fishing, or just lounge in the shade of a palm tree, Desert Oasis is the place to do it.*

Southwestern Floating Island: *Not even the Tostarenans know how to reach this floating island in the sky, but art lovers the world over believe there's a connection with the Lake Kingdom.*

Tostarena Ruins Entrance: *Goombas, Bullet Bills, and cactuses too! The Tostarena Ruins aren't the safest place in Sand Kingdom, but they sure are neat.*

6

Tostarena Ruins Sand Pillar: If you've ever wanted to a see quicksand, a sand geyser, or a whirlpool of sand, this is the place to come.

7

Tostarena Ruins Round Tower: The jumping off point for fans of extreme sports. Capture the Glydon and take flight. Can you fly all the way to the fountain in Tostarena Town?

8

Jaxi Ruins: Adventurers discovered the top of the ruins by way of a pipe leading from an underground ice cave. How there came to be a Jaxi Stand in such a hard-to-reach place is anyone's guess.

9

Moe-Eye Habitat: *Can you see what the Moe-Eye sees? If not, you must not be using their special sunglasses. The stone giants are gentle, but timid, so do be considerate.*

10

Tostarena Northwest Reaches: *The far corner of the desert is a great place to rest. Or, if you're feeling spry, to try a Freerunning Race.*

Getting Around

Sand Kingdom offers a couple of different options for getting around besides Mario's own two feet. Warp Points are the fastest way to travel, but taking local transportation is half the fun of visiting a new place.

Spark Pylons: *Leave it to those ambitious Tostarenans to string electrical lines throughout the kingdom. Put Cappy to use and zip along on the wires connecting the many buildings and ruins.*

Jaxi: *Can you spare 30 coins? If so, visit any of the Jaxi Stands scattered around Sand Kingdom, request a Jaxi, and hop aboard. Jaxi is extremely fast and can run through—or over—just about anything. But he can be tough to steer. Be ready to press those brakes!*

Souvenir Hunting

If there's one place where you're sure to get some good local souvenirs and an outfit to match the local style of dress, it's in Tostarena Town. Scour the landscape for 100 purple coins in the shape of pyramids and spend, spend, spend!

CRAZY CAP: TOSTARENA EXCLUSIVES	
ITEM	**REGIONAL COINS**
Sombrero	5
Poncho	10
Cowboy Hat	20
Cowboy Outfit	25
Sand Kingdom Sticker	10
Jaxi Statue	5
Inverted Pyramid Model	25

HAZARDS & HOSTILES

The desert is harsh: the heat, the lack of water, the mummy-like creatures that prowl the dunes at night. Sand Kingdom is home to a number of hazards, including two creatures that can cause trouble for wayward wanderers.

GOOMBETTES IN LOVE

Not all Goombas are dangerous. The female of the species vanishes if approached, but not if you approach as a Goomba. Capture a Goomba and head to either of the two Goombettes to sow the seed of love.

Goomba: *Goombas confine themselves to the Tostarena Ruins, but they're mighty protective of their home turf. Whatever you do, don't try taking their hat.*

Chincho: *These mummy-wrapped creatures only come out at night, so take a Jaxi if you leave the safety of town after dark.*

Bullet Bills: *Bullet Bills also prowl the Tostarena Ruins. Thanks to Cappy, Bullet Bills can even double as a source of transportation!*

Poison Wastes: *That purple lake around Jaxi Ruins and in the Moe-Eye Habitat may look like grape-flavored taffy, but it's no sweet treat! One step is all it takes to knock a visitor out.*

Quicksand: *The sand inside the Tostarena Ruins is on the move, and it's looking to take you with it! Visitors better stick to the solid ground.*

LIZARDS IN THE RUINS

The Tostarena Ruins aren't just home to large creatures. Visitors have spotted lizards scurrying about as well. Rumor has it that some of them carry coins.

CAPTIVE FRIENDSHIPS

Not all of the Sand Kingdom's inhabitants are hostile. From the local Moe-Eye to the area's visiting fisherman, to the high-flying Glydon, Mario can capture a number of neutral creatures. Each of these captures has a unique ability that makes your time in the desert all the more enjoyable—and memorable. Don't pass them up!

Lakitu: Lakitu and Mario haven't always been the best of friends. Fortunately, Cappy is here to smooth things over. Toss Cappy at Lakitu to do some fishing with him at Desert Oasis. Rumor has it that Lakitu may even uncover an old friend buried in the sand.

Moe-Eye: The Moe-Eye don't like to be disturbed. In fact, they're terrified of most visitors. But not only do they pose no threat, their special sunglasses can be used to see the otherwise invisible. Capture them to see the world like never before!

Glydon: High atop Round Tower is a mighty lizard known as a Glydon. Mario can capture this winged friend and soar across the desert. The Glydon can't gain altitude as it soars—it's a Glydon not a Planedon—but it can be used to glide from ruin to ruin, covering great distances with each leap.

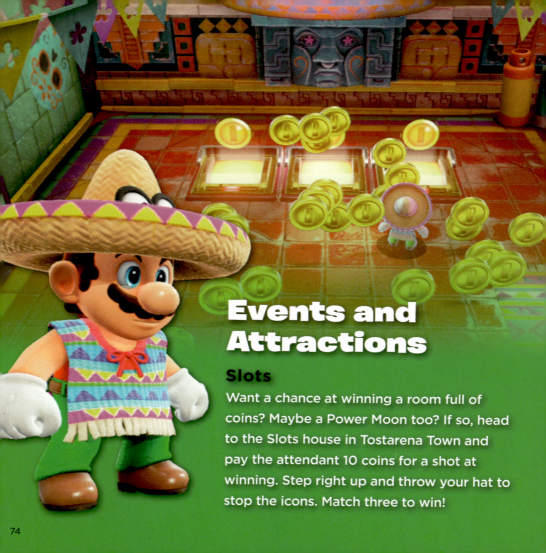

Events and Attractions

Slots

Want a chance at winning a room full of coins? Maybe a Power Moon too? If so, head to the Slots house in Tostarena Town and pay the attendant 10 coins for a shot at winning. Step right up and throw your hat to stop the icons. Match three to win!

Private Club

The Tostarenans certainly like to entertain their out-of-town guests, but they have a saying: Dress like us, party like us! Buy a Poncho and Sombrero from Crazy Cap to gain access to a special dance club on the northwest of Tostarena Town. Don't be shy! Make yourself at home on the stage and watch as Mario strums a nice little ditty.

Koopa Trace-Walking

Walking isn't just good exercise, it can be competitive too! Talk to the Koopa northwest of town and test how well you can walk in a perfect circle. The Koopa shows you the path, but his arrows soon disappear. Can you walk like a true champ?

100 points!

Koopa Freerunning

Enter the race in Tostarena Northwest Reaches and get ready to race clear across Sand Kingdom! Entrants in this race have it easy: they get to ride a Jaxi! Mario is in no risk of pulling a muscle as he zips to the finish line in style.

Postcards with Peach

Peach sure does know how to travel. And she's not afraid of heights either! Meet up with her atop the Inverted Pyramid for a classic Tostarenan photo-op overlooking the desert expanse.

Trivia Time with Sphynx

Head on over to the Sphynx on the north side of Tostarena Ruins to engage in a bit of question-and-answer. The questions are multiple choice, and the Sphynx likes it when people guess (no, he doesn't).

Art Appreciation

Ever see a painting so lifelike that you felt like you could just fall right into the world? There's a painting just like that on a pillar west of the ruins. Go ahead, take a closer look.

Local Advice

A Dash of 8-bit Patience

There are two essential ingredients to a fulfilling 8-bit experience: patience and speed. Visitors looking to experience the area's intriguing 8-bit architecture should wait in a safe place before changing direction or leaping to a higher level where new threats may exist. Study Goomba patterns, then act. Fast!

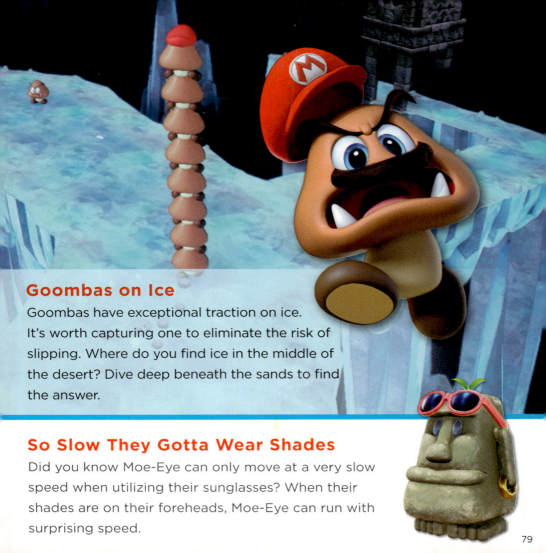

Goombas on Ice

Goombas have exceptional traction on ice. It's worth capturing one to eliminate the risk of slipping. Where do you find ice in the middle of the desert? Dive deep beneath the sands to find the answer.

So Slow They Gotta Wear Shades

Did you know Moe-Eye can only move at a very slow speed when utilizing their sunglasses? When their shades are on their foreheads, Moe-Eye can run with surprising speed.

Kingdom Adventures

Travel Companion Volume 1

Written by Doug Walsh

DK/Prima Games, a division of Penguin Random House LLC
6081 East 82nd Street, Suite #400
Indianapolis, IN 46250

© 2017 Nintendo

ISBN: 9780744019308

Printing Code: The rightmost double-digit number is the year of the book's printing; the rightmost single-digit number is the number of the book's printing. For example, 17-1 shows that the first printing of the book occurred in 2017.

20 19 18   4 3 2

001-310362-Oct/2017

Printed in the USA.